BEYOND THE BULLRING

JULIE BODEN

INTRODUCTION

HELENA RUDGE

BRIAN LEWIS

PONTEFRACT PRESS
2001

Publisher: Pontefract Press
17 Linden Terrace
Pontefract, WF8 4AE
01977 793121
pontefractpress.demon.co.uk

Distributors: Water Tower Distribution
PO Box 9480
Sutton Coldfield
West Midlands
B76 9RN

© Text: Julie Boden
© Cover Photos: Richard Battye
Editor: Brian Lewis
Cover Design: Harry Malkin

Production Team: Reini Schühle and Margaret Morton

Printer: FM Repro, Liversedge

ISBN: 1 900325 19 5
CD Recording available: CELCDJMB219

Thanks to Brian Lewis for bringing this book to life.
To Reini Schühle, Richard Battye and to Harry Malkin.
To my family, these poems are mere tokens of the love I owe
and in this book the answer to a question begins.

To John,
my husband, my love, my rock
and the whetstone of my mind.

CONTENTS

On Selecting Poetry for Review

Grand Union

M6 - Southbound

Birmingham Northern Relief Road

At the Dog and Doublet

The Big Black Dog

Temptation at Digbeth

Balsall Heath Bedsit

The Bank Restaurant

Espresso

Despatch from The Royal Arch

Response to The Royal Arch

Up Rosemary Hill

Beyond the Bullring

Conversation at the Cock Inn

Mirror

Moth Screams in Suburbia

Good Hope

For My Brother Peter

Bracebridge

The Burntwood Piano Tuner

A-Z

My Piano Lesson

Beyond the Bull

The Stranger Came

Volvox Verses

FOREWORD

She loves him in the Sutton Coldfield way,
between the avocados and the tricksy crème brulée.

This first collection of Julie Boden's poetry speaks from the urban heart of Birmingham. It takes a fresh look at a city, which is constantly reinventing itself. She is a true poet of place, writing her city into life, with humour and charm.

Her skill as a poet allows the reader to journey through the alienation of urban life, to emerge with hope for the future. The poetry is multi-dimensional, and stretches the reader in the true Bardic tradition. This does not make the poetry inaccessible but, like the experience of seeing precious seed pearls warming on the skin of a beautiful woman, is something that the poetry reveals quite naturally.

The pace of city life is echoed in her more postmodern texts such as *Black Dog*, where the rhythm of the poem beats like the healing drum of a shaman to take the reader on a dreamlike quest for spirituality. But as the second half of the collection reminds us, it has to go *Beyond the Bull*. The book is grounded with a strong sense of reality that searches beyond the face. As a teacher of English, Philosophy and Drama, Julie understands the need for clarity and artistic interpretation.

The poetry speaks with an honest voice, which refuses to patronise the reader. It manages to elevate the every day out of the mundane, in true Wordsworthian style, revealing the uniqueness we so often miss in our ordinary lives:

Let other Bards of Angels sing,
Bright Suns without a spot
But thou art no such perfect Thing;
Rejoice that thou art not!

William Wordsworth

Julie's text also refuses to accept that only the apparently beautiful things in life are fit for poetry. She writes about a remembered journey on the *M6 Southbound*:

One star upon a faultless sky
and half a moon to journey by,
a hypnotising drone of cars
and lights that pass in fits and starts
to blind us from the road ahead.

Having seen Julie perform these poems live, I had some reservations as to whether or not the cadences might get lost in the written form, but was pleasantly surprised to see the finished article. This is clearly the result of many hours of careful craftsmanship, and an instinctive knowledge of how poems work.

We make no apology for having both a foreword and an editorial to this book. Each has a different job to do in relation to the text. We hope you will have as much pleasure from this collection as we have had reading and compiling it.

Helena Rudge

INTRODUCTION

I heard Julie read her poetry aloud before I read it in manuscript form, it was a powerful performance. The first poem I heard was *Grand Union (A Canal Sestina)*. Solid in-your-face verse, it caught and held your attention. Structures were recognisable, word play well considered and her keen sense of craftsmanship evident.

The occasion was the meeting to award the fifth Birmingham Poet Laureate. In the interval I found myself standing next to her in the coffee queue and discovered that she had written since she was a child, though with increasing enthusiasm in the past five years. Last year she won the City of Birmingham Poetry Slam. Julie is a founder member of Poetry Pals, who run poetry workshops in schools around the City. In later conversation I discovered that she was taking an M Ed at Birmingham University.

I spent a pleasant evening in the company of someone I liked, and it would probably have stopped there had I not left my spare poet's satchel in her car, when we all adjourned to the Duke Inn. I had never taken in her second name, and I knew next to nothing about her. The satchel, like Basho's, was care worn yet had little sentimental value. However Julie tracked me down, thinking that I might need it.

On the day I got my satchel back I asked to read more of her poetry. Publishing was not mentioned, although she knew that I very occasionally published poetry.

We slowly drifted into an understanding that I would act as an editor, not just as a proof reader, and that her first collection would come out under my imprint, Pontefract Press.

I am very interested in 'poems of place' and she had written a number of these, so they became a scaffold. But from the first we knew that other poems would enter the collection as we felt fit, and this proved to be a good decision.

***

Why do I like Julie Boden's work? I like it because she is full of surprises, and challenging. You can read a controlled piece where tradition is acknowledged both in title and in form - *Grand Union (A Canal Sestina)* - and then flick forward and find a loosely structured piece, brimming with passion and imagery such as *Temptation At Digbeth*. Performance pieces, full of wit and force, though invariably deserving a close read to allow sampling of grace notes, sit beside ones which need quiet contemplation. Then again she is not afraid to be lyrical and touch areas of experience which are universal and timeless. The setting for *One Star* might be the *M6 Southbound* but it also has echoes of deserts and tundra.

At every turn the poetry is an expression of her life. We hear about the family, the children have dedicated poems, and a brother, husband and parents are celebrated.

> *My brother chooses lines that sound like songs.*
> *My husband dares not tender his advice:*
> *Poems are like dresses – dodgy ground;*

Following close on the line 'sex is a sneeze/a nose to blow' (*Balsall Heath Bedsit*) is, 'the seconds pass/the veils are down/ Herodias – three minutes.' Such literary allusions may send you to a good dictionary, perceptive imagery. The reader is never patronised.

Then there is her love of Birmingham and its people. This is absolute, but often comes in the dry humour I associate with the city. My uncles quietly mocked themselves - I do that too - and I see it as a strength. I suppose it takes one to know one.

And last of all: Julie Boden is never self-congratulatory, never says, 'look at me, I am a poet.'

That is why she is one.

Brian Lewis

ON SELECTING POETRY FOR REVIEW
To Sophie Hannah

Ten or fifteen of the best, you said,
as Mr Bumble flexed a silent cane.
Truth is relative and so is Art.
And all my relatives have staked their claim
(or so it seems).

The honest, caring verse that always rhymes
my mum would choose as best without a doubt.
My son prefers the ones he understands.
My daughter chose reflectaphors:
the symbols of mind that do not scan... but resonate.

My brother chooses lines that sound like songs.
My husband dares not tender his advice:
poems are like dresses - dodgy ground;
a man, when pushed, may mutter, 'Very nice.'
(Mine does it blindfold).

Ten or fifteen of the best, you said.
My hand still fears the striking of the cane.
If Art is Absolute and this Pure Crap
then Plato is the man that I shall blame.
But if all shit is relative, perhaps
I'll ask for your opinion just the same.

GRAND UNION
A Canal Sestina

This tale begins upon a cold canal.
A barge of people hurrying to bring
their story of a stranger or a pal,
adventure of a pauper or a king.
By Birmingham, not Canterbury, each shall
have told a tale of person, place or thing.

The journey starts. All strangers. Not one pal
to travel with. As lonely as a king.
Each traveller stares into a cold canal
and wonders at the message he may bring.
Stares out into darkness where he shall
catch fish tales of some dreamy dreamed up thing.

They tell and in the telling is the thing.
Mumbling through nervous coughs they shall
never reach a listener's ears unless a pal
strains hard to hear the subject of his king.
What presents do these modern magi bring
who travel, not by camel, but canal?

The royal barge - a body. Each man king
of his own fate. He travels the canal,
trapped between the tow paths of this thing
cut out by man - some long lost navvy pal,
who thought his sweat brought progress. Did it bring
it? Each man thinks he does. But what man shall?

What tales of life can this year's pilgrims bring
to Birmingham, by barge, on cold canal?
No Wife of Bath, no Miller, no great king
of faith to serve. They search to find a pal.
Elusive happiness, that special thing,
can it be found? They hope... but doubt it shall.

We travel onwards hoping that we shall
one day find the story that will bring
a sense of purpose, friendship, love... a pal
to journey with. A queen for every king.
Our Holy Grail? The key to life's canal
that unlocks all the secrets of the thing.

The ordinary pal, the mighty king
hope to bring it back, but what man shall
find the thing to warm this cold canal?

M6
SOUTHBOUND

One star upon a faultless sky
and half a moon to journey by,
a hypnotising drone of cars
and lights that pass in fits and starts
to blind us from the road ahead.

Beyond a screen of conifers
the distant city lights shine out.
Upon the crowded motorway
with stiffened backs and aching necks
we weave our way across the night
and try to shut the madness out.

Half a moon to travel by,
A star upon a vaulted sky.
A beam to catch the traveller's eye
beneath the evening's closing eye.
An engine's throb, a throttle's cry,
a scream of traffic charging by
and there, upon a darkening sky,
One star.

Λ star.
An angel's twinkling eye.
Two thousand years are rolling by
with half a moon and half an eye
to cast upon the darkening sky,
One star.

As western wise men journey by
they wander on,
we wonder why.
They look upon their sign and sigh.

One Star.

We wander on,
we wonder why.
We look to find a sign.
We sigh.

Weave a way beneath
a half lit sky

One star.

BIRMINGHAM NORTHERN RELIEF ROAD
For Nathaniel and Charlotte

Shepherd's Cottage has been brought to bricks,
a broken shell of mortar, dust and dirt.
Bill Lowe's farm has tape you cannot cross
disclaiming any fault for public hurt.

Wishaw church rings out a silent bell,
a vicar talks of ashes... dust to dust.
A bird flies off, an acorn finds a wind
to carry it and hopes for soil to trust.

Knowing they can enter any day
we treasure every moment they don't come,
a toll that we must bear; no choice. We pay.

They cut another motorway in Brum.

One day soon no one will look at this,
the shed that houses left-overs of lives,
the rockery we broke our backs to build
some twenty years, or so, ago.

Soon they will be bulldozed from our lives.

One day soon no one will smell this earth,
the field fresh ploughed, the honeysuckle gate.
I photograph each blade of grass of you
to keep you fresh, before it is too late.

We stand beneath the shadow of *The Oak*
and rest against the sorrow of its trunk.
Soon our hearts within its life are felled.
A scar of motorway on sacred ground,
a stall of traffic coughing junk will come

that doesn't by-pass hearts.

AT THE DOG AND DOUBLET

Waiting on the falling sun
we enter our last lock,
pull the great barge in
and dock beside an inn
that welcomes us.

Genies corked in bottles
queue on shelves.
Thudding darts miss the eye
seek out the double top.
We top up drinks
drunkenly attempt to find
one tow path in the dark.

Beneath an amber light
patterns petiolate and green
drip down their red and black.
Something sinister, surreal
thrown in a warming warning light.

We throw our insides out
throw up,
throw down our clumsy bodies
into sleep.

Hung up on the morning
we will seek small trinkets out:
find empty vessel ornaments
to decorate,
watch small enamelled
Romney brushes
paint out rosy castles
in the dark.

THE BIG BLACK DOG

On city streets they walk the big black dog,
on city streets they shop the big black dog,
through city tunnels drives the big black dog,
city tunnels choked by big black dog.

City people
walk the big black dog.
City people
talk the big black dog.
City people
walk the big black dog.

In their beds they cry the big black dog,
on their pillows dream the big black dog.
Disco beating, panting big black dog,
dancing and romancing big black dog.

City people
walk the big black dog.
City people
talk the big black dog.
City people
walk the big black dog.

In city parks they chase the big black dog,
in city parks they shit the big black dog.
Old cathedrals leaping big black dog,
spires and towers pawing big black dog.

In the city
life is inside out.
In the city
life is inside out.
In the city
faith is turned to doubt.

Country people knew their big white god,
in their fields they walked their big white god,
in their forests fought for big white god,
serfs and children talked to big white god.

In the car
the mirror is reversed.
In the mirror
white god is reversed.
In the city
black dog is rehearsed.

Temptation at Digbeth

For Sale

Animals
dead animals
dead bits of animals
dead

block-chopped
'reduced while stocks last'
animals
shelf-laid
sealed inside a shroud
meat
untainted
animals

The Temptation

I will the flood to stop inside my mouth,
the juices not to rise.
Salivatory expectation is a strange lip-licking thing
that makes us bite the apple and be damned.
And so I leave my memories behind,
the smell of fun and feast.
Instead, I feel the fragile bones
that we have wished upon,
tiny broken carcasses
where voiceless wishes snapped;
where wishes
snapped.

DRIED OUT PREACHER

An ex-meat junkie, craving gastric juices of another life
fills his plate with foreign vegetation,
preaches the new gospel of a meatless man:

'You shove your hand into a creature's arse...
and call it seasoning.
You cut a cow in two and call that murder
"Art", swallowing your lies in vintage wine.
It's time to tell the truth of it
the knuckle part
the tender bit
this napkin has a knot in it.
You must remember them.'

THE FLOCK

This year I will remember them.
This year I will not eat their meat.
This year... there must be groups that I can join,
some therapy to change this man for good:
a group where I can testify,
'My name is Judas,
I am a carnivore!'
a priest to whom I can confess,
'I've tried the pills, the potions,
patches placed on legs,
on breast;
but, Father I just seem to crave meat more.
...must I go cold turkey?'

FOR SALE

Meat untainted
shrouded
bits of animals
'reduced while stocks last'
animals
dead animals
dead

BALSALL HEATH BEDSIT

The buzzer rings
three minute call
to curtain up
to curtain fall
there really is
no time at all

Three minutes

She boils an egg
she will not eat
sex, premature
and incomplete
lies out upon
a dirty sheet

Three minutes

The grains fall down
and scratch the glass
the hours come
the seconds pass
the veils are down
Herodias

Three minutes

The doorbell rings
another bloke
walks through the door
through city smoke
another daughter
learns to choke

Three minutes

Sex is a sneeze
a nose to blow
he cannot stay
he turns to go
through hoary frost
on fallen snow

Three minutes

She holds no wine
she tips no glass
the hours come
the minutes pass
her life is dull
her world is crass

Three minutes

She grips the mug
she gulps cold tea
the time has come
and so has he
another man
another fee

Three minutes

Fast food sold
on busy street
back street boys
are indiscreet
young girls gag
on rotting meat

Three minutes

Sex's a sneeze
a nose to blow
solicitation
fellatio
no talk of Mike
or Angelo

Three minutes

She breaks the shell
but where's the joke
the doorbell rings
another bloke
and all her dreams
go up in coke

Three minutes

The buzzer rings
three minutes call
from curtain up
to curtain fall
there really is
no time.

THE BANK RESTAURANT

Monday, rain day, eighteen year day
since me white dress, horse shoe gay, day.
Monday, rain day almos' flood day,
card and flower day, meet 'n' treat day.
Monday, joke day, Noah' flood day,
two by two go to de Bonk day.
Monday go day, make a change day,
two by two in moving glass day.
Laugh-n-squeeze day, body-tease-day,
body move in movin' glass day.
Mirror door and wall t'see day,
Feng Shui hidin' toilet shit day.
Chardonnay and goat cheese grill day,
braise roast lamb and rosemary mash day.
Business men in suit dat lunch day,
business men dat chew de cud day.
Mobile phone dat throb and ring day,
tree wid colour cube te fit day.
Sunshine picture on de wall day,
egg box ceilin', pack dem in day.
Backgroun' jazz and trumpet blow day,
porthole window, seasick loo day.
Talk o' pas' n' VSO day,
loss ambition, dream dey go day.
Pay de bill and tank de Bonk day,
come day go day, leave de ark day
Monday, rain day, eighteen year day,
linen white and sail away day.

ESPRESSO
Brindley Place Café

Espresso Number One
(They sit)

Espresso Number Two
(He talks)
Sugar cube unwrapped she watched it slip and slide
jump out into a cup
splash suicidal sweetness up.

Espresso Number Three
These cups, he says, are made for dolls
one's not enough to wet your lips
don't they know some men prefer a mug?

(He exits)

Espresso Number Four
He called a spade a spade.
Her macho man.
No gushy words or gondolas for him.

Espresso Number Five
Was it so little time ago that she had glowed post-coital,
blessed that Eden-Venice for her luck...
before the death his words had brought - this builder of
the Crosby homes that rise from city muck.
He had known the stuff that dreams were laid upon,
while she must learn to call a fuck a fuck.
Mouthing out her pain against an Evesham cup, even now -
she could not say -
the 'F' word.

Espresso Number Six
Pulling out the insides of a thing with straps
she felt an invitation: formal, black.
Fingers riding out the dark waves cut along the side of it
she reached to find a lipstick,
paint a face to face another Poppy Ball.

In this second city mock Venetian square
where folksy barge turned gondola
she raised an empty cup.

'*Ancora ...un espresso... per favore.'*
The waiter, picking up the crumbs that other mouths had
dropped, moved
between the tables
like a crow.

Espresso Number Eight
Somewhere else a figure slipped into a cold canal,
left a life unnoticed.
Save perhaps, the startling of a bird...
a small worm
dropped.

Espresso Number Nine
The woman stirred a spoon to struggle sweetness in
pushed down her feet
raised up her chin
sent a silent order to the crow.

And when the cappuccino came...
revelled in the chocolate and the froth.

DESPATCH FROM THE ROYAL ARCH

I've joined the 'City Living Set' in Brum.
I have no time to think, no need to cry.
The money from the settlement has come.
It seems you'll find life hard, much more than I.

I know my lawyer had you on a spit
that turned you on your words until you roasted.
She proved beyond a doubt that you're *a shit*.
I don't know why I try to keep you posted.

The head-hunters have found me I'm afraid.
Oh, what a happy victim I've become.
Much under worked and grossly overpaid,
reporting on the social scene in Brum.

My city office has no view of you.
My penthouse at 'The Royal Arch' is built;
designed with garden you won't need to do.
But nor will I. So kiss goodbye to guilt!

If you'd like to keep in touch - then read the 'Post'
unless these days you'd rather have a Mail.
I'm pictured in 'Post People,' dining out,
paid to find the gossip, tell the tale.

I have no time to write and so goodbye.
your baggage at this Mailbox, love...
is sorted.

RESPONSE TO THE ROYAL ARCH

Dear Sir,
If some young frog should come to call,
before she tears his legs off for her lunch,
could you not write Health Warnings on the wall.
(We frogs are such a poor endangered bunch.)

Tell him, 'Do not kiss this poor princess
with bright red lips designed to drive you mad.
Her lips are gates that suck you into hell.
Go buy yourself a single lily pad.'

I've moved into a quiet tranquil pond.
I have a secret 'men only' address.
The only rabbiting we hear is frog.
There are no bloody women to impress.

PS: I understand you have my bag,
a worn and grubby thing that's been revamped.
The faulty fastener cannot be zipped up,
it's filled with junk, I wish I'd had it clamped.
Lock it up somewhere and lose the key.
I know that you'll regret it if you don't.

Up Rosemary Hill

Jack and Jill
moved up the hill
as fast as Jill could push him.
Jack felt down,
he worked in town.
The job did poor Jack's head in.

Up Jack got
at five o'clock
into the rush hour traffic.
Jill had not
his dinner got,
Jack's language, it was graphic.

Jack and Jill
moved up the hiill
as fast as they could caper
to hide the cracks
of worn out smiles
behind designer paper.

Then one day
Jack ran away.
He said he couldn't hack it.
He had to flee
Jill's PMT.
She took him for a packet.

BEYOND THE BULLRING

She loves him in the Sutton Coldfield way,
between the avocados and the tricksy crème brulée.
Her love is organised in such a certain Sutton way,
she loves him in the Sutton Coldfield way.

His love is of the Little Aston kind,
a Roman Road; a journey with a settlement to find,
an Aston Martin he adores but has to leave behind.
His love is of the Little Aston kind.

Their love's a frozen Four Oaks strange façade;
kippers, curtains, games of bridge (a bluff with every card),
where keeping up appearances is hard.
Their love's a frozen Four Oaks strange façade.

Her diary leaves so very little space
(to pen him in). There is no place
for him in her mad chase
to find herself. Her diary leaves him... verylittlespace.

CONVERSATION AT THE COCK INN
Response to a friend's adultery

Your head has gone and turned upon your heel
with Love, or Lust by any other name,
I do not understand the pain you feel.

I tell you that your mind is all that's real,
the bomb will not explode if you don't go.
I do not understand the pain you feel.

I make one last unwelcome sense appeal
to change your mind. You walk out, starry-eyed.
I do not understand the pain you feel.

You cheat upon your partner with a meal,
a sperm-choked lunch and half smoked cigarette
and afterwards, you learn of pain for real.

You turned your back on truth and hoped to deal
a hand of cards where jokers weren't allowed.
I do not understand the pain you feel.

You argued once that thoughts are just as real
as acts. So it was futile, stifling desire.
My thoughts are dragons slain upon my steel.
You do not understand the pain I feel.

MIRROR
Moxhull Hall

Here
against the wall
stands a silent witness.
Door of the Past
a cold, clear eye,
unyielding.
Priest of many confessions
receiver of the sly side glance
rehearser of the unrehearsed.
Patiently waiting
at this spot.
Venerated
by so many acts
of private devotion.

MOTH SCREAMS IN SUBURBIA

All night they heard the moth
and, with the moth,
the ticking of the clock,
the planes that flew upon their nightly path,
the scratching in the loft of claws on wood,
the hegdehog's click,
the sudden screams of cat.

None of this had troubled sleep before.
Those piercing screams
had not kept them awake.
The rape cry of the vixen come on heat
was natural,
the screeching owl,
a friend.

But words invoked the furies from the ground
and wind threw up a blast upon the house.
The rain, the driving rain, grew fast and loud
and drove its bullets on the groaning house.
They did not sleep.

All night they lay awake within their beds
where words had flown
on moth wings from her mouth.
The creaking house repeated all the words
that echoed back,
from East, West, North and South.
They did not speak.

The kamikaze words flew on all night
around them and the light inside the hall.
Their children found no comfort there at night,
those moth wings burnt her words upon the night.
She wished each syllable could be unsaid,
but on they fluttered, fluttered into light
and flew around each restless, sleepless head.

None shall sleep now... none shall sleep now...
Now none shall sleep, they said.

When, in dawn's light, she rose to change her clothes
she cried to see the damage that was done:
the backless, sexy jumper when they met,
the Aran she had worn as dressing gown,
the négligé in amber tones and jet,
the tiny, white embroidered christening gown,
the black chiffon, the tracksuit for the park;
her life, in clothes, lay ruined in the dark.

Each garment showed the fretting of the moth, where
Words had eaten memories.
She did not know that words could fly like moths,
she did not know,
'I did not know,' she said.

GOOD HOPE

Do not throw crumbs of promises
or feed me with your lies,
your kindly words of good intent
are merely a disguise.

Don't hide behind your learning,
don't feed me truth in grains.
If the body of your knowledge fails,
don't feed me the remains.

Arm yourself with arrogance,
smile and play the clown
feed me with placebos
if you want to push me down.

But if you want to help me
then just put away your pride,
hold my hand with honesty
and be a faithful guide.

Perhaps then with some dignity at death
I'll close my eyes.
But while my mouth belongs to me I say,
'Don't patronise.'

FOR MY BROTHER PETER

Three months after the funeral, an optician said:
'Your pain is due to unshed tears.'
He did not know that at Dad's passing
floodgates opened and the safe, strong shutters
came crashing down.

We are the same tree, you and I.
Born of the same wood,
struck by the one blow.
We are the same tree, you and I.

In the rings of our years
simply read this:
'We are the same tree, you and I.'

BRACEBRIDGE
For Lucy

Pushed out like a sleigh one May morning.
The dry land would not carry you.
In the stillness of your birth
my heart felt the coming of Winter.

Since then, each year, as snowdrops bow
and laughter sings between the trees
I walk the Bracebridge walk beside the lake
that helps, somehow.

In Derbyshire, upon those Stepping Stones,
we waved your ashes back to find the sea
and in the years that pass I welcome back
the tiny cloud white memory of sky.

If, in the tiny promise of your life,
if parts of you have helped another live
then there is something else that we can bless.

Only, let them hear the music of your life,
the music tiny organs might have played
before they take the knife.

THE BURNTWOOD PIANO TUNER

The piano tuner came one day
Post-Christmas, Pre-Millennium.

'These days are strange,' he said,
'a limbo land where dogs must still be walked
and Christmas lies behind us like a death,
and not a birth.'

He spoke, then lifted up the lid
fresh-shaved of ornament
and peered upon the hammered brain.
His fingers felt for problems
hidden in the ageing frame.
He pointed to the springs long gone,
the many signs of strain;
expressed a need to take away
the heart of it, re-thread the loops,
remove it to a workshop, Burntwood way.

Then blindly reading thoughts that hung in air,
he said, if we preferred, we could make do.
He would not carry music out, play bearer at a funeral.
He would not leave an empty shell at all.
He tuned it best he could, hoping it would hold.
We moved outside to stand and wave our visitor away;
and the notes were almost perfect.

The notes were almost perfect.
For a day.

A-Z

Somewhere after Abberley, before Zorrina Close,
flicking through an ageing A-Z;
he dreams of turrets built on concrete towers
where windows open up a greener view
to scenes where pastoral knights ride pastel horses,
dragon-breathing mortals mock no knights
and no one pokes a finger at the Grail.
Somewhere in the depths of Abberley,
somewhere in that distant Abberley
dungeon keeper secrets hide no tale.

Somewhere, here, before Zorrina Close,
he hears the papered secrets in the walls,
punching bass notes pound his ceiling in,
drawbridge faces hide their almost smiles
and he turns down a battered A-Z,
turns the dog-eared, dog-tired pages down.
He will not miss the urine on the stairs,
the strange graffiti traps that bring him down.
He shapes the city clouds into his form
then jumps and falls to sleep as traffic stops.

From A, the apple promise he can't keep,
to Z, the final sleep. The final sleep.

MY PIANO LESSON
For Charlotte

Soaking in a morning bath
I heard Charlotte
playing the piano:
surfing keys,
riding octaves,
swallowing the foam
and laughing,
playing the piano with a passion.

That day, there came a new precision.
Movements, slow; exact.
Her expert eye explored each tiny error,
began again, began again relentlessly.

My waters chilled
as each new scale was climbed,
notes rolled out like waves
beneath her fingers.

Lying in the shallows
I heard a calling.

You grow towards me
interplaying discipline with pleasure

and turn my frozen water into wine.

Beyond the Bull

Beyond
Beyond the Bull
Beyond the Bull Ring noise of it,
      the Hockley centred calf of it,
      the Mammon munching crisp of it,
      dog cannibal and shit of it,
      the rat race, fast lane pit of it,
      the gunshot, phone-mug hit of it
a resonance still rings in it.
A resonance still sings
Beyond
the Bull.

THE STRANGER CAME

The day the stranger came
I did not recognise him,
recognise her,
recognise the way of things,
the shape of things,

I did not understand the form at all.

I stood before the door and there arose a haze
yet not a haze,
a thing
quite like a haze
that rises from the hottest desert floor.

And through it came a thing of white,
of light.
that walked
and yet it did not walk.
That glided.
Yet it did not glide.

But passed... and did not look at me at all.

Love, in a breeze, passed through me,
a peace,
a sense of purity.

There rose a swell
of certainty
no dictionary defines.

And through it all
there rose a frame:
a simple frame,
where all this crazy, complex world made sense
and death became an enemy no more.

The thing left me without a name to call it by,
passed through the gate inside the hedge's wall.
When suddenly, like Lawrence at his snake,
I threw a rod of doubt at it,
for though the thing was wondrous strange
I was afraid that words would never be enough
to tell the truth of it.
And people would consider me a fool.

Film upon my lenses broken down like crazy paving,
eyes all dry and sore.
Even then I did not tell the truth of that strange heat,
for what was there to tell?

A thing
without a name
had come and gone
and left all things
much as they were before.

I've thrown a thousand stones since then,
to frighten off the thought of it.

But, though I try to classify this thing as myth
and messenger or angel as mere words
invented once upon a time by man,
I find I never can escape the form of it.

'Seek not to Understand that ye Believe,
First Believe that ye may Understand.'

What words are these? An empty sound,
ridiculous and trite.
How can they help the honest man
whose quest to know the way of things
relies upon his questioning?

And yet... what if it's true?
It may be right.

That form moves on beyond the word,
beyond both day and night.

VOLVOX VERSES

Within the orchard of a house I know
there is a tree
full boughed and Eden bright
heavy with a fruit
whose ripeness calls.

Bare figure
on a distant hill
reaching for the stars
and touched by lightning,
charred bark
fingers still and black
a statue set against a closing eye.

Loneliness is near and never far
in waters of the flesh and of the sea
where clichés spat upon an echoed wind
rise up again to form some constancy.

All is transient and passing strange,
passing strangers find new rooms to view
where wordless echoes fasten to the walls
and move to block the viewer from the view.

Word-hooks hang the veilings of our thought
between the known, the unknown and the odd.
Nonsense, sense and no sense fill the gaps
with muslin metaphysic nets of god.

Before what will be
after all before
we jam a life
between a closing door.

A wave packet
is wedged upon the shelf
behind the clock that ticks away the time.
Schrödinger's cat, a zombie on the lap,
is dead, yet lives, is live, but not alive.
Capra called this zombie form a dog,
but all the barking sounded in his head,
and so with nothing certain anymore
we take a walk with Heisenberg instead.

All things passing strange will strangely pass.
The modernist, not modern anymore,
will scratch upon the blackboard of a life
and shed its skin in chalkdust on the floor.
Professors nailed to ageing desks will write
their crosses in a futile tic-tac-toe
where logic leads to stalemate every time.
The four line grid can hold no moves
these logical professors do not know.

Heidegger and Sartre stand alone
en-soi, pour soi,
poor sods they can't avoid
the nihilistic floodgate breaking through,
the Age of Space
becomes
An Age of Void.

In Hereford, a map describes the world
as centring around Jerusalem
but modern scribes say it expands from mind;
so does my world expand from Birmingham?

Concentric, ego-centric circles form
where particles, like Garbo, stand alone.
We find the particles and ride the wave,
tear off the skin
chew marrow out of bone,
but do not see the fractal of the fact
by counting circles on an ice cream cone.

All is paradox and paradigm,
an age of alienation, not of space.
And like a stranger on an unknown shore
where foreign tongues call out to foreign faces
we try to find a place to rest awhile
to peel beyond the face behind the faces.
Beware the concrete cat upon the mat

whose hairs you split with drill-eyed questioning,
blinded to the abstract in the act
we miss the meaning of the living thing.

Separateness is but a point of view.
We come together though we dance apart.
The Wu Li dancers dance, and yet do not;
theirs is a tantalising tantric art.

Lonely is the heart without the face
that comes by night, in dreams, but not by day.
Lonely is a buried mandolin,
a Grecian girl who hears its ghost strings play.

Lonely is the song that isn't heard,
the man who stands outside
but not by choice.
Lonely is the page without the word,
lonely is the word
without the voice.

Loneliness: Empirical and real
is found upon the journey in and out.
We fill our days with axioms and truths
and wrestle with the lonely night of doubt.

And so your loneliness is yours alone,
you house the bones your body has to chew.
We weave a path, uncharted, without form.
You join a dance that always played in you.

We separate like Volvox,
yet, do not.

Thoughts it seems are word-wings of our flight
and words in flight
mere words
are all we've
got.

Julie Boden

Born Julie Davis, in Sutton Coldfield, England, in 1960, Julie has lived in the West Midlands region for all of her life. Educated locally to degree level she married John Boden in 1982. Since her marriage she has combined her educational career with bringing up their family and the demands of hotel life. While completing her M Ed at Birmingham University she is also working as a specialist visiting teacher, a poet in education (PIE) and a freelance advisor. Julie is a member of Combination Poets and of the Sutton Coldfield Poetry Society. As an active member of Poetry Pals she conducts workshops in Birmingham schools and she is also on the editorial board of the new Millennium Artists Press. Last year she was the city of Birmingham Poetry Slam Champion and was invited to read to groups in the city's libraries. She performed at the Midlands Arts Centre and in the Birmingham Arts Festival at the invitation of Simon Pitt, the Birmingham Poet Laureate. This year she was shortlisted for the Birmingham Laureateship herself. Her poetry has been printed in *Raw Edge* and award winning poems have been published in anthologies. This is her first collection.

Helena Rudge

Helena Rudge, born Dublin, Ireland, 1951. Graduated Birmingham University with a BA Honours in Literature and Language. She has had her poetry published in *Raw Edge* and is a member of Poetry Pals providing workshops for schools.

Brian Lewis

Born 1936 in Birmingham, this teacher, critic, painter and publisher has lived in Pontefract since 1960. He was Birmingham's first Poet Laureate in 1996 and two years later Deputy Chairman of Yorkshire Arts. He is currently Director of Tutorial Delivery for the Open College of the Arts and Visiting Fellow in Verse & Fine Art at Loughborough University. He has won the Raymond Williams Community Publishing Prize for a book about a women's prison. He is currently co-ordinating a series of projects on arts and housing in Bolton.

In 1992 Brian Lewis and Reini Schühle founded *Pontefract Press* so that they could publish quality community books and fine art editions.

Richard Battye

Born in Wakefield 1963, Richard graduated in the Midlands in 1986 in Visual Communications. He assisted in photography studios before setting up River Studio in Birmingham, an advertising/commercial studio, in The Custard Factory in 1990. Clients include Gibson Guitars, Land Rover, Birmingham Children's Hospital, Halifax Bank. Work has taken place all over the UK and in France, Spain, Dubai, and Los Angeles.

His large touring exhibition, *This England*, a celebration of the individual, has led to several exhibitions and is still growing. Richard also lectures in partnership with Kodak. Work can be seen at *www.riverstudio.co.uk*